Georgia Society

Address of Colonel John Screven

Georgia Society

Address of Colonel John Screven

ISBN/EAN: 9783741124389

Manufactured in Europe, USA, Canada, Australia, Japa

Cover: Foto ©Lupo / pixelio.de

Manufactured and distributed by brebook publishing software
(www.brebook.com)

Georgia Society

Address of Colonel John Screven

ADDRESS

OF

Colonel John Screven

DELIVERED AT THE

FIRST ANNUAL DINNER

OF

The Sons of the Revolution

ON

February 8, 1892,

AT

SAVANNAH, GEORGIA

FOREWORD.

THE Society of the Sons of the Revolution, in the State of Georgia, was instituted in the city of Savannah, on the 22d day of May, 1891, and is required, by the terms of the 14th By-Law, to hold an Annual Meeting on the 5th of February, in every year, except when such date shall fall on Friday, Saturday or Sunday, in which case the meeting shall be held on the following Monday. The 5th of February was chosen to commemorate the adoption and promulgation of the first Constitution of Georgia, in the year 1777. It is a further standing regulation of the Society that the

members shall, when practicable, hold a Com-
memorative Celebration, and dine together at
least once a year. Accordingly, the date of the
first Annual Meeting was also made the time for
the first social gathering of the Society's members.
The dinner was given at the De Soto Hotel, and
the tables were set in the banquet-room in the
shape of a diamond, with the space in the centre,
representing a star, in the midst of which was a
profusion of potted plants, the edges being trailed
with running vines.

The Society then numbered seventy-seven members, of whom thirty-seven occupied seats at this,
its first dinner; and, by a happy thought of one

of that number, this brochure, containing the first speech of the occasion—that of the Society's President, Colonel John Screven, in response to the toast, " The Sons of the Revolution "—has been prepared and printed in this elegant form as a souvenir of the occasion, the edition being limited to the number of members subscribing to the dinner.

To the thoughtfulness and liberality of Mr. Wymberley Jones De Renne, great-grandson of the Honorable Noble Wymberley Jones, who, during the struggle for American Independence, was "conspicuous for purity of purpose, wisdom of counsel and fearlessness in action," are we indebted for this beautiful specimen of the printer's art, which is, at the same time, a pleasing reminder of a most enjoyable event in our Society's history.

WM. HARDEN,

Secretary.

SAVANNAH, GA., February, 1892.

SONS OF THE REVOLUTION.

Gentlemen :—In endeavoring to respond to the first toast of the evening, "The Society of the Sons of the Revolution," I will confine my remarks to a brief exposition of the objects and value of this honorable association.

This society having adopted the constitution of the general Society of the Sons of the Revolution, their objects are identical, namely : " To perpetu-ate the memory of the men who, in the military, naval and civil service of the Colonies and of the Continental Congress, by their acts or counsel, achieved American independence, and to further the commemoration of the anniversaries and the prominent events connected with the war of the Revolution ; to collect and secure for preservation the traditions, rolls, records, and other documents, public or private, relating to that period ; to inspire the members of the Society with the patriotic spirit of their forefathers, and to promote the feeling of friendship among themselves." To become a member of the association taking such high trusts in its keeping, the constitution provides that "any male person above the age of twenty-one years, of good character, and a descendant of one who, as a military, marine, or naval officer, sailor, or marine, in actual service under the authority of any of the thirteen Colonies or States, or of the Continental Congress, and remaining always loyal to such authority, or a descendant of one who signed the Declaration of Independence, or of one who, as a member of the Continental Congress, or of the Congress of any of the Colonies or States, or as an officer appointed by or under the authority of such legislative bodies, actually assisted in the establishment of American independence by services rendered during the war of the Revolution, became thereby liable to conviction of treason against the government of Great Britain, but remaining always loyal to the authorities of the Colonies or States, shall be eligible to membership in the Society."

A WIDER ORGANIZATION.

I have thus taken the liberty of presenting these clauses of our constitution, in order that such gentlemen as have not had access to the text itself may have clear apprehension of the purposes of the Society and the necessary qualifications of its members. Hitherto the only association in this country intended to promote the same objects is the Society of the Cincinnati, whose membership, so far as Americans were concerned, was wholly confined to commissioned and brevet officers of

the army and navy of the United States. This
limitation of membership to a circumscribed class
of the patriots of the Revolution may have been
justly adapted to the conditions of the times in
which it was established; but it barred from ad-
mission to the order all others of the patriots of
the Revolution, whose services were as essential
to the cause of American liberty as those of the
commissioned officers of the Continental or United
States Army. Civil officers of the State or Colonial
governments of the most eminent character, distinguished for great abilities, for severe personal
sacrifices, and unstinted devotion, without whom
any form of government or political organization

and the conduct of the cause itself were impossible, were excluded. So, too, the non-commissioned officers of the Continental Army and of the State militia were ineligible for membership. Sir William Napier, the distinguished author of the history of the Peninsular War, wrote that the humbler classes of a nation are always the most patriotic in time of war. In no instance was this more signally true than in the American Revolution, when the farmer, who shouldered his musket and went to the front, left his home to be plundered, his family to almost certain suffering and want. Throwing out of view the great fact, that armies and navies are of the people, and without the people are impossible, who will venture to deny the individual valor of the soldiers and seamen of the Revolution—the seamen of Paul Jones, Barney and Nicholson—the soldiers of Washington, Gates, Greene, Lincoln, Wayne and Marion; and if we turn to our own beloved State, whose ravaged soil was red with blood from Augusta to Sunbury, the impetuous soldiers of James Jackson, who won the keys of Savannah.

A PUBLIC INHERITANCE.

This grand inheritance is wholly public—an inheritance in which all the people of this great country are coparceners. But the members of this society have an inheritance peculiarly their own, as the blood descendants of the men of the Revolution. Enough has been said of their achievements; but it seems, as of course, that the duty of gathering and perpetuating the records of their careers, whether public or private, should devolve upon their descendants, wherever these records are as yet unsystematized and unwritten— a duty attaching to all classes, whether eminent or humble. It is in vain to assert that history contains all that is necessary or interesting to be known. History deals with facts pertaining to nations, seldom with those relating personally to individuals, while it is true that civil or military bodies are but aggregations of individuals. It must, therefore, be also true that the conduct of such bodies will depend upon the motives, character and actions of their individual components. If there is anything true or good, anything great or exalted, in the motives and actions of the revolutionary sires, their sons have a right to claim them, not with misplaced or insolent boasting, but with "secret joy" and a grateful sense of potent obligations to recognized good examples. We well know and sadly deplore the difficulty of securing such records—a difficulty which began with the Revolution itself; when even the public records of our own State were secretly moved from successive hiding-places until at last they found refuge in distant Maryland; when such private records as were not destroyed by the torch of the enemy were ransacked and flung to the winds, if they contained no evidence of so-called treason. It is impossible to estimate the ravages of this nature when Provost made his raid into South Carolina in 1779, when pictures were the special objects of destruction, and so the portraits of many distinguished patriots lost to posterity. This difficulty will increase with advancing years; and now, before the worm and the damp, those stealthy assassins of time and death, shall have obliterated them forever, let us rescue the too long-hidden records of our sires, that we may prove to the world not who or what we are, but who and what they were, and the illustrious examples they have bequeathed to succeeding generations.

A RIGHT TO BE PROUD.

It must be acknowledged that the descendants of revolutionary sires have some right to entertain just pride in their ancestry as the founders of American independence and as the oldest tenants of American soil; but it should be clearly and emphatically understood that the Sons of the Revolution are not tainted with the aspirations of aristocracy. In examining the membership rolls of the Sons of the Revolution in the State of New York it was, therefore, not surprising to find that, of 707 members, 158, or over 22 per cent., were the descendants of non-commissioned officers and private soldiers. Of these, four were officers, who have the same equal rights with descendants of generals and signers of the Declaration of Independence. No democracy could be purer, none more levelling ; and so the descendants of Apollus Austin the fifer, of Philip Schuyler the general, William Floyd the signer, of John Jay and Alexander Hamilton, all claim alike the honors and privileges of " the Society of the Sons of the Revolution."

And now, gentlemen, a few words in conclusion. The last and crowning injunction of the constitution of our society is the promotion of a feeling of friendship among ourselves. When the great bard of Chios chanted the challenge of heroes, he sang :

> " Each other's race and parents well we know
> From tale of ancient days ; altho' by sight,
> Nor mine to thee, nor thine to me are known ;"

and so, although we have never in the flesh beheld our forefathers, yet in the mind's eye we may conceive of their lineaments ; and if there is the heredity, in which we may indulge a reasonable belief, I feel that we see something at least

of their lineaments in the members of this honorable company. They were comrades in the times
that tried men's souls, bound together by ties of
singular sacredness ; and even now, when a century has passed over the scenes of their trials and
their triumphs, and their bodies are but dust, it is
well for us not only to cherish their noble memories, but to feel that they have also handed down
to us and to our posterity the tender heritage of
their friendship.

THE VALIANT JASPER.

In this same city, within short bowshot of the
spot where Colonel Walton with his one hundred

Georgia militia held the rear of the American line until the forces of General Howe had passed in disorder and panic—within short bowshot of that spot is erected a monument of bronze to the heroic memory of William Jasper, a simple sergeant in the Second South Carolina Regiment, a soldier without a commission, but the fame of whose career has passed to all the borders of this vast country; whose name identifies public places, towns and counties, and has a page in universal biography : yet neither the descendants of this illustrious exemplar of American valor and patriotism nor Sergeant Jasper himself, had he lived, could find a place in the only association hitherto dedicated to the sacred memories of the Revolution! So, too, the heroes of the transcendent victory of King's Mountain, where nine hundred of the sturdy yeomanry of the Alleghanies, hitching their horses at the foot of the mountain, and advancing (every man for himself), slew and captured eleven hundred British regulars and tories. On this occasion Colonel Cleveland, when about to lead his division to the attack, told his men that "every man must consider himself an officer, and act from his own judgment. . . . If any of you are afraid, such have leave to retire, and they are requested immediately to take themselves off." And yet neither Campbell nor Cleveland, Shelby, Scott nor Williams, all of whom were colonels, but of militia, nor the brave yeomen who were to consider themselves officers—those noble citizen-soldiers who had brought hope and fresh courage to the American cause, then sinking to despair in South Carolina— nor any of their descendants, could be enrolled in the Olympian sanctuary of the Cincinnati.

It is very far from my purpose or desire to depreciate the high merits of the Society of the Cincinnati. Organized in 1783, by officers of the Revolutionary Army of the United States, to per- petuate their friendship, and to raise a fund for the relief of the widows and orphans of comrades who had lost their lives in the war, its objects

were of the most exalted character, and should
have forbidden such an American as Benjamin
Franklin to fear that it was the initiation of a
future aristocracy. But what was Achilles without his Myrmidons, Alexander without his Mace-
donian phalanx, Cæsar without the Tenth Legion,
Napoleon without the Imperial Guard, or Washington without the ragged but indomitable militia,
who sprang up from the Piscataqua to the Alta-
maha, and with their bloody bayonets laid the
foundation of this transcendent republic ?

A NOBLE PURPOSE.

And so "The Society of the Sons of the Revolution" has been organized to supply a deficiency

akin to national in its demands, to fulfil a duty which in times past was either neglected or impossible, and, before it became too late, to reestablish and effectually perpetuate the memory of the services of all classes of patriots who loyally served in any capacity, whether civil or military, the cause of American liberty. Nor is this an expression of mere sentiment in its common acceptation, although it has been said that sentiment moves the world. The whole American people, but peculiarly the posterity of the bold and devoted patriots of the Revolution, owe them an inestimable debt. It is not all that they bared their breasts to the storm of battle. It is no enough that they staked their fortunes in the conflict. It is not enough that they suffered intolerable privation, want and indignities. It is not enough that they were scarred not only with wounds of sabre, bayonet and bullet, but by ignominious fetters. It is not enough that so noble a man as Isaac Hayne perished as a felon; nor that their great leaders, such men as Washington, Adams, Jefferson, Madison; nor that Bulloch, Habersham, Jones and many others of our Georgia sires were liable under British law to indictment for high treason and to death upon the gibbet; but look around you, sons of revolutionary fathers, upon the priceless inheritance they bequeathed—a country, whose boundaries are almost continental, whose territory teems with great cities of vast foreign and domestic commerce, connected by a system of unequalled internal and foreign transportation; with a population twenty times greater than that of the revolutionary period, living under a political constitution enacted by the fathers, and which, after the lapse of a century of trial, their happy posterity have seldom ventured to amend—a land of such beauty and plenty, of such security, prosperity and peace, that it is sought of all the peoples of the earth! Look around you, sons of revolutionary fathers, and answer whether the perpetuation of the memories of the men who handed down an inheritance so illustrious, so sublimely positive in its reality, is founded in a sentiment of unsubstantial value, and not in lofty truths as immovable from the hearts of men as the seated hills !

The Sons of the Revolution

IN THE

STATE OF GEORGIA.

FIRST ANNUAL DINNER

SAVANNAH, GA., FEBRUARY 8,
1892.

Menu

BLUE POINTS ON SHELL

HAUT SAUTERNES

CLEAR GREEN TURTLE, AUX QUENELLES

VINO D'PASTO

CELERY   OLIVES   TOMATOES

BOILED RED SNAPPER, SAUCE HOLLANDAISE   POMMES PARISIENNE

SADDLE OF VENISON, LARDED, SAUCE GRAND VENEUR
FRENCH PEAS   MUSHROOM A LA CREAM

PONTET CANET

FILET MIGNON, SAUTE BEARNAISE

STEWED TERRAPIN A LA MARYLAND

ROMAN PUNCH AU KIRSCH

ROAST QUAIL BARDES ON TOAST

MOET & CHANDON WHITE SEAL

LETTUCE SALAD

NESSELRODE PUDDING
PETIT FOURS GLACE   FRUIT   CHARLOTTE RUSSE
COFFEE

THE DE SOTO

REGULAR TOASTS

1. THE SOCIETY OF THE SONS OF THE REVOLUTION:
   COL. JOHN SCREVEN, of Savannah,
   President of the Society in Georgia.

2. THE FIRST WRITTEN CONSTITUTION OF THE STATE OF GEORGIA:
   HON. HUGH V. WASHINGTON, of Macon.

3. THE UNITED STATES OF AMERICA.
   HON. EMORY SPEER, of Macon,
   Judge U. S. Court, So. Dist. of Ga.

4. THE DAUGHTERS OF THE AMERICAN REVOLUTION:
   COL. JOHN MILLEDGE, of Atlanta,
   State Librarian, Historian of the Society in Georgia.

www.ingramcontent.com/pod-product-compliance
Lightning Source LLC
Chambersburg PA
CBHW021621290326
41931CB00047B/1394